"There are people halfway around the world in Bangladesh that Joe will never meet – yet he serves with an open heart. Joe understands that when we lift up one family, we are lifting all families. He is modeling the behavior of our Lord and Savior, Jesus Christ: food, clean water, clothing, healthcare – these are all things Joe has provided through his support – and what is evident to those served is that someone truly cares about them – someone miles and miles away – and they are so grateful."

– NANCY JERNIGAN, DIRECTOR OF PARTNERS IS SUSTAINABLE DEVELOPMENT

"Joe has been the source of inspiration to all of his classmates through his incredible leadership and generosity."

– BOB SCANLON, McBRIDE CLASS '69

ESTO
VIR

PRAISE FOR THE AUTHOR

"Every moment that I have shared with [Joe]— in formal and informal settings—has made me a better person and leader. His strong beliefs, convictions and spirituality always make me stop and reflect. . . And his ethics have always been the rock-solid standard that all could be guided by."

– DIRK BEVERIDGE, COLLEAGUE AND FRIEND

"The proof of the pudding. Look at Joe's achievements with family, business and charity."

– ANDREW WUELLNER, CHAMINADE '76,
SAINT LOUIS

"I wanted to let you know the profound impact Joe's involvement has had on me. His generosity and commitment have inspired me to review my life and reflect on all I have to be thankful for. My McBride education laid the foundation for my college education; I attribute my success to attending McBride. . .Joe's inspiration has also made me realize the importance of paying it forward, leaving a legacy, and serving God, family, church, and community."

– ED BOVIER, CLASS OF 63' MCBRIDE LEGACY
SCHOLARSHIP FUND STEERING COMMITTEE

"The best part of having known Joe all these years is the connection and trust we developed along the way. He is a good person that has always put his family, friends, and co-workers before anything else."

– CARL WAY, COLLEAGUE AND FRIEND

"Several things have made a deep impression on me. The way in which Joe values his Catholic Marianist education is truly striking. The goal of all Catholic education is to form good Christian people and Joe is a wonderful example of the realization of that goal. His values and outlook on life received some of their clearest embodiment in his approach to life. I don't think I've ever met anyone who understands more profoundly the gift that you were given."

– FATHER RALPH SIEFERT, FORMER CHAMINADE COLLEGE PREPARATORY SCHOOL PRESIDENT

"Joe is a natural teacher, always eager to offer his help and insight. Besides his business expertise, I was drawn to his people-focused approach to business and his perspective and encouragement gave me more confidence. It was that coaching that helped in the formation of our Watlow Way company culture which has had had a lasting impact on me and everyone associated with Watlow."

– PETER DESLOGE, COLLEAGUE AND FRIEND

"Joe's generosity is amazing, but more importantly, his passion, commitment and love for McBride is palpable. McBride was a special place. The education and the values that we received there gave us all a great foundation to build our lives."

– JOHN MARINO, MCBRIDE CLASS OF 1970

"I got to know Joe and his commitment and dedication to McBride High School, the Brothers that taught him, his family, men and women who have served our country of which many never came home, his faith, and his commitment to help others receive the opportunity he did at McBride. His combination of humility and generosity are hard to find in one person, but Joe has a ton of both."

– MIKE HAGENHOFF, MCBRIDE CLASS '63

ESTO VIR

STORIES OF A MAN GROWING IN
FAITH, FAMILY, DUTY, AND HONOR

JOSEPH NETTEMEYER

THRONE
PUBLISHING GROUP

Lead Writer: Paul Chaney
Editor: Kendra Paulton
Cover and Internal Design: Heidi Caperton
Proofing Editors: Earl Menchhofer and Vicki Rich
Publishing Manager: Tim Jacobs

DEDICATION

I dedicate this book to the women who shaped my life. My mother, Marcella "Sally" Nettemeyer, and my grandmothers, Josephine Pingsterhaus and Elizabeth Nettemeyer. They were tough-minded women, shaped by World War I, the Great Depression, World War II, and the Korean War. They understood struggle, the need for faith, perseverance, their responsibilities, and they never shrank away from them. They also understood the need to develop those traits in a boy, and they never veered from their expectations or living a life of example.

The other most important woman in my life is my wife, Jane. We have been together for forty-six years. We have shared life's challenges together, standing shoulder-to-shoulder as a team. She has inspired me to get up every day and give my best effort. I believe God directed us to one another. She has been and is my most precious blessing.

TABLE OF CONTENTS

FOREWORD

Many times over the years, I have listened to my father tell us about his experiences growing up, describing himself as "just a poor south St. Louis boy trying to make a living." He always spoke fondly about relations among family members and the importance of faith and serving God, often concluding that he would like to, someday, write a book detailing how those experiences shaped his life.

Growing up, my father maintained high expectations of me, my sister, and my brothers. He expected us to keep up our grades, help around the house, and be involved with our church and community. Laziness was not an option.

During my childhood, our family made four major moves across state lines. Although these transitions were tough at first, we became resilient in learning how to manage change. My parents upheld a stable household, and they demonstrated love to God, each other and us. They worked hard as a team, and although money was tight at times, we never felt deprived. As a result, our family became dependable, and we still hold a close bond into adulthood. We learned to trust and rely on each other. We learned that friends come and go, but family is here to stay. With the recent death of my grandfather, my father's recovery from a minor stroke and bypass surgery, and unexpected major medical diagnoses among other immediate family members, the self-examination that accompanied it sharpened my interest in understanding our family history. This ambition became more pressing for my dad as well. He began to write down his story, starting with his childhood, his entrance into high school and college, forward into the early days of his marriage, and finally into the times of my childhood and afterward.

The result is a very personal story. It is the story of one man's life and ambition. It is about the family and the childhood that shaped his dreams, about pivotal experiences that sharpened those dreams, and about the struggle to fulfill them. It is the story of an honest man.

For my part, I hope this will help my children understand some of what came before their own struggles with life. Someday, they too will want to ponder where they are going and from where they came. In a time when age-old wisdom and grace are needed, I pray this testament resonates to young men and women to build their house upon a rock.

ANNE (NETTEMEYER) VRANICIC
APRIL 26, 2021

THE STATE OF MANHOOD TODAY

Today, society and culture are sending many wrong, convoluted messages about manhood. Young men, especially, lack clarity in who they are and their role in the world.

They misunderstand what manhood is really all about. They put a priority on temporal, material things and are taught to have a selfish heart — to enjoy life but not take on the responsibilities that go with it. They want material things but don't understand life is about so much more. They are not hearing the lesson of giving back, sacrifice and serving others for a higher purpose. It's all about "me" not "we."

Today's generation of young men needs a change of mindset. They must believe they can make a difference — not with grand gestures but a willingness to sacrifice comfort to help others and contribute to society. To be givers, not takers. To give more than they receive and give others a hand up. Ultimately, to become part of a community of contributors.

The greatest threat to the character of a young man today is to be seduced by the easy way out. The great things in life

— faith, family, duty, and honor — require commitment to rise to the challenges that life brings to your doorstep. A good life is built by not shirking from those challenges. The worst habit a young man can develop is taking the easy way out. That type of habit impairs the potential and the quality of life that they can achieve.

Don't be seduced by easy!

INTRODUCTION

This book has a single purpose: to help young men understand what manhood is all about. The title, Esto Vir, is Latin for, "be a man."

In the chapters that follow, I aim to encourage, embolden and empower intentional discipleship among young men, to deepen their commitment to Jesus Christ, to their families, their church, and community, and to demonstrate their faith in the everyday activities of life, both at work and home.

I want to present a vocabulary of masculinity and teach what manhood is all about using my story as a template. I do it with straight talk, pulling no punches, without sparing your feelings — not without compassion, but as a father to a son. Throughout the book, I talk about my father's impact on my life, making me the person I am today.

My goal is to provide opportunities for you to have a hand up, to give you hope that you can be more than you think, to escape your self-limits, and to understand that fear is a subtle, invisible chain that shackles you to an "I can't do it" mentality. I want to move you from "I can't" to "I can." It is a path out of cynicism to, "you can make a difference."

You can waste your time with negativity, or you can approach life positively. You can be a man, meet your responsibilities, and honor your commitments for a higher purpose than self-satisfaction or personal gain.

Nothing worthwhile in life comes easily, including growth into manhood. It comes from perseverance and personal aspiration. The status-quo doesn't last. Once you get content with the state of your life, you're a target. You have to step past the fear of living within your comfort zone. Only then will you experience real growth.

The architect Daniel Burnham put it this way: "Make no little plans; they have no magic to stir men's blood and probably themselves will not be realized. Make big plans; aim high in hope and work." The message is, don't live your life small and selfish. Live your life large, and let a generous heart be your guide.

Finally, let me assure you it is okay to be a man, even if culture and society say it's not. Permit yourself to lead, be self-confident, and have a vision for what you can achieve.

Esto Vir — Be a Man.

CHAPTER ONE

THE BRICK HOUSE

FAMILY, THE BUILDING BLOCK OF SOCIETY

Family is the foundational building block of society, and the family unit is integral to a healthy community. When a man and woman form a family within the bounds of their faith, it becomes the motivation they need to make a difference for their children, community and society.

Families contribute to the welfare of society by having a code of conduct and setting an example. They are involved in activities that make their communities better. Whether through their church, civic groups, charitable organizations, or schools, their participation and outreach help the community thrive.

Stable families aspire to have their children do well. They optimize educational experiences, promote physical development, volunteer in different ways to provide opportunities for children to grow and have the best quality of life possible. They share a common set of values, like a magnet that pulls them in the same direction.

Every generation comes into the world thinking that what they're experiencing is what the world sees for the first time. That's not the case, of course. Older generations help the younger understand and gain a broader perspective — good is not always there forever, and neither is bad. They help them understand that life is not always an upside but can confidently say that this, too, shall pass. Families provide the assurance they can get through whatever life throws their way, together.

In 2010, Jane and I established a charitable trust fund, the Nettemeyer Generous Heart Fund. The fund's mission is to identify programs that provide opportunity for children to advance their skills and education.

Each year, Jane and I give our children, nephews and nieces a set amount of money from the trust to fund educational programs for disadvantaged children. Our niece Jenni (my brother Mike's daughter), introduced me to Boys Hope Girls Hope, an organization that finds young men and women who have the potential to complete college but have personal life situations that would prevent them from ever realizing that opportunity.

The program, run by fellow Catholics, identifies these talented individuals, and through their network, supplies a safe living environment, tutoring and admission into Catholic high schools in the St. Louis area. The organization's board members engage in fundraising to support this opportunity. Their success rate at getting these young men and women into college is commendable, a direct result of committed men and women of faith going the extra mile to help these talented individuals realize their full potential.

This program is an example of how like-minded individuals can come together to make a difference in someone's life. We are happy to be a contributor to their efforts.

Another group I am involved with, Breakthrough, in Silicon Valley, works with young Hispanic men and women to give them opportunities and get into college. As with Boys Hope Girls Hope, all of the people working in the program are from strong family backgrounds.

My point is that families are the nucleus of support that builds a better nation by providing opportunity, balance, safety, and stability. Strong societies evolve from healthy families.

FAMILY, THE BUILDING BLOCK OF MY LIFE

When my first daughter was born and the nurse handed her to me, everything else in life took on secondary importance compared to the opportunity I wanted to provide for her. That has been my purpose for forty-one years for each child who became part of our family. I determined long ago that I would get up every day to do everything I could to help them discover their full potential.

My son was asked once about what it was like growing up with me as his father. He paused for a moment and said, "He has high expectations of us and never compromised on them. We have all accomplished more than we ever thought we could, but that was because he never compromised."

My desire to provide opportunity for my children was handed down by my parents. My mom and dad were Great Depression farm children, and to them, family was everything. They came together to survive, support each other, provide for their families, and give their children opportunities they may not have seen themselves.

Our mantra was "family first." "Friends come and go, but family is forever," Mom and Dad always said. I have a much deeper appreciation for that sentiment the older I get. We are there for each other, to lift up one another.

My parents married after my dad got back from serving in World War II in 1946. My father did not want to follow in his family's footsteps and go into farming. Instead, he and my mother moved to St. Louis, and Dad became a streetcar conductor with the transit authority. At the same time, mom did piecework at the Brown Shoe Company.

They first lived in a basement apartment that opened up into an alley. There was such a housing shortage that mom and dad were grateful to get any place. Then, they moved into another modest apartment that overlooked the Anheuser-Busch brewery. I was born during that time and lived there for several years. We then moved into another, bigger apartment consisting of three rooms and a large closet in the front, where I slept.

Mom and Dad saved all the money they could to buy a home. Mom brought home improperly-sewn piecework — wallets, purses and other leather goods — to repair in the evenings. Dad had moved from the streetcar to driving a bus and worked as much overtime as he could. He took a second job on his days off to set aside even more.

I was six years old when my parents bought their first home, a tiny brick house in an urban St. Louis neighborhood they purchased for forty-five hundred dollars. Even though it was small, it was, for my parents, the ultimate achievement. They had been saving for years to make enough money for the down payment.

My dad, along with his brother and brothers-in-law, overhauled the house to improve it. They put in a new bathroom, replaced the heating from a coal-fired furnace to natural gas, tore out the kitchen, and rebuilt the cabinets. They took a structure that was in rough shape and turned it into a home. The shared sweat of family made it possible. Days in our household started early. After a breakfast that typically consisted of oatmeal or Cream of Wheat, my job as the oldest was to make sure my brother and three of our neighbor's children got to and from school on time. We lived about a mile away and walked every day, rain or shine.

We had Mass every morning, then classwork, and were done around three p.m. I would gather up my brother and head home. That experience started giving me the responsibility of being a shepherd.

Dad was working split shifts. He would get up at four-thirty in the morning and work the rush hour, be off, and then work the evening shift. Being home during the day, Dad would cook, as Mom got home about four-thirty each afternoon. We always had a parent there when we went home. We were each given chores and responsibilities and had to get them done by dinner. Every member had to contribute to the success of the family.

We had dinner as a family whenever we could, when Dad's work schedule didn't conflict. In the evenings, he taught us card games, helped us with our homework and otherwise engaged in our lives.

That was our week during the school year. We spent weekends on the farm, visiting family and helping out. That fabric of providing support was woven into my life at an early age.

I am part of a large family. I have forty-eight first cousins from both sides of the family, and to this day, we're still very supportive of one another. We relive youthful misadventures and have some good laughs, too. They have been part of my life for the past seventy years.

Even though my immediate family and I now live thousands of miles apart, I'm amazed at the interaction my four children have with their cousins. They get together, travel together, and support each other when someone is struggling. They are there for each other because, like me, they understand that's what makes up a family's fabric.

THE BLESSING OF FAMILY

One memory remains etched in my mind that serves as a clear example of our family coming together to support one another.

One summer day, my younger brother Mike had gone bike riding at a local park with a group of friends. As they were crossing Kingshighway Boulevard, a major thoroughfare, a car crossed over into the parking lane and hit my brother.

Mike was rushed to the hospital, where he was diagnosed with a fractured skull. Things were touch-and-go. My parents couldn't afford around-the-clock care, so Mom would go to the hospital after work and spend the night. My aunt would come early in the morning, and Dad came later after he finished the morning shift.

My dad was trained as a medic in the Army during World War II. One day, as my brother was sleeping, Dad checked his pulse and found it was weak and inconsistent. Dad immediately got the nurse, and the medical staff rushed in and brought him back to consciousness. Had they not, he would have passed away, the doctor said.

Today, Mike is a very successful businessman with three children and five grandchildren. Had it not been for my father's medical training or instinct to check him regularly, my brother would not be with us. That is the blessing of a family — to provide support and safety in good times and bad.

Sadly, my father passed away thirty-four years ago and my mother, ten. But a child blessed with such good parents never shuts them out of their thoughts.

People may believe that time will develop a scab over the wound of loss. I never wanted that to be the case with me. I am not saying that I wanted the pain to remain raw and unchecked; I wanted people to understand how important my parents were to me. Every breath, every step, and every action I take is a testament that bears witness to their importance. Without my parents being who they were, I would not be who I am.

LESSONS LEARNED FROM FAMILY

Growing up in a family like mine, you learned many lessons. For one, my parents had expectations. They expected their children to be people of faith and involved in our parish. They expected us to work and taught us how to contribute to the welfare of the family, the community and the organizations and associations to which we belonged. However, their greatest lesson was teaching us how to pray; the commitment to prayer is a thread that has run throughout my entire life.

Our family had strong values. Good enough wasn't good enough. If we were capable of getting "A's" in class, we better get A's. They taught us to push past our self-imposed limitations. We did not want to disappoint Mom and Dad or bring shame to them. That's still with me today and has been a source of personal motivation that speaks to how highly we thought of our parents.

They didn't coddle us; they pushed us. They taught us to do the right thing and to honor our commitments. They would say the only thing of value you have is the commitment you make, and you see it through no matter the cost. I've made some commitments that I questioned but saw them through in tribute to my parents and the lessons they taught me.

That's why families are so important. They teach us value systems. They help us discover that we can be more than we think. That's how I pursued my entire life.

LESSONS FOR YOUNG MEN

Whether or not you are a young man who has the benefit of a good family, you can put the following lessons into practice.

Join a community of like-minded people. They become your support group. They will set examples for you that you can emulate. Find those groups that help you discover and aspire to be a better person. The church is one such place. You will find people there who aspire to live by a higher value standard. Become an active participant, not just a passive spectator — you get nothing out of it by remaining inactive. Take on the responsibility to challenge yourself to make a difference and learn in the process.

Don't just talk about your faith; live it. Embrace Christ's most important message: Love one another. Provide those who have a sense of hopelessness with hope. Through your compassion, live the message of Christ. A quote attributed to St. Francis of Assisi says, "Preach the gospel every day and use words when necessary." Show by example how we can be better.

Find your uniqueness, your special ability. That will propel you on a quest for a better life.

Learn to give generously. A lesson my grandmother taught me is that the key to a happy life is a generous heart. You get more satisfaction out of giving than receiving.

Have the mindset that your past doesn't have to determine your future. Even if you have been disadvantaged, you can change the course of your life. Aspire for something higher.

Do the right thing. What is accomplishment? It's not degrees behind your name, not career success, recognition, or awards. It's about getting up every day and doing the right thing by God, your family, church, community, and work. Surround yourself with people who do the right thing.

Find a mentor. I'm a big fan of mentorship and have had that opportunity many times with family members. For example, I have one nephew who is a successful businessman. Every month, he calls me to get my input on business issues and affirmation he's doing the right thing.

As a member of the Texas A&M School of Industrial Distribution Advisory Board, I have had numerous opportunities to counsel students looking for guidance on building a career. I've helped them make connections to be successful. The biggest challenge we all have is overcoming our self-imposed limits due to our fears ruling us. A mentor helps someone get past their fears.

Become a contributor and avoid the takers. Last, surround yourself with contributors, and help those who genuinely need help, but don't give takers your time. They will suck the life right out of you.

REVIEW QUESTIONS

1. What was it like to grow up in your family?

2. Describe one specific time when you felt your family's support.

3. What is one lesson your parents taught you that impacted your life in a significant way?

CHAPTER TWO

Open Arms and Opened Eyes

I have eight grandchildren. Most go straight to their grandmother when they visit, but one certain grandson comes to me to snuggle in his grandfather's lap. Of course, I greet him with open arms. That's not unlike how the faculty and students treated me at McBride, the Catholic high school that would help set the course for a lifetime of faith.

Here's my story.

In 1964, students who desired acceptance into one of the Catholic high schools in St. Louis had to take a test to determine how well they comprehended the material. The Diocese had decided students would fall into one of three tracks: A, B or C. Track A consisted of students with accelerated comprehension; Track B, those with average understanding; and Track C, students whose grasp was slower.

My score listed me as an "A" student. As a result, I qualified for two boys' college preparatory high schools: St. Louis University High School, run by the Jesuits, and McBride, a Marianist school. St. Louis University High School accepted me. A short time later, my parents got a call from the school administrator, a Jesuit priest, for a meet and greet.

At the meeting, he shared a dilemma. An alumni member had a son who wanted to get in, and some current students with siblings who didn't score as high as me also wanted in. The priest made this recommendation: accept an offer from the other school, McBride.

My parents' perspective was that you qualified based on your credentials, the school's on who you knew. A school I was more than qualified to attend rejected me, favoring those who were less so. It was the first time I was confronted by such prejudice — not being chosen based on merit, but relationships.

To my good fortune, McBride wanted me. They wanted to know my interests, aspirations, classes I liked, and what I enjoyed reading. Two individuals met with me the day of my visit, the outgoing student body president and the incoming president. They spent time with me, saying they viewed me as a contributor to the school. One school rejected me based on *who* they knew; the other accepted me because of *what* they knew about me.

After my acceptance, there was consistent communication from the administration. My parents and I also met with the faculty in small groups, who engaged us from the very beginning. However, the most significant selling point to my parents was when they told us, "If you give us your son, he will come out and be a man."

LIFE AS A MCBRIDE STUDENT

At the center of the McBride campus was a magnificent three-story, colonnaded building located on the corner of Kingshighway Boulevard and Easton Avenue (now Martin Luther King Drive) in the heart of St. Louis. It was built in the mid-1920s by the Catholic Diocese of St. Louis with funds donated by the McBride family to honor William Cullen McBride who died unexpectedly at a young age.

Each of the students in my class came from strong Catholic families. We had attended Catholic elementary schools across St. Louis, went to mass five days a week, and, thus, were steeped in the church's traditions. That laid a foundation for our faith on which McBride built.

The school consisted of a bunch of smart teenagers — high IQ individuals, some with IQs over two hundred. We called ourselves "Micks." Out of my class of one hundred fifty-two students, we graduated scientists, researchers, university professors, CEOs, doctors, attorneys, politicians, and clerics. Not bad for a group of working-class kids who were realizing potentials we didn't even know we had. I have to give credit to the priests and brothers. They established expectations to help us focus on achieving our potential.

My classmates and I bonded tightly. If someone needed something, we would rise to the occasion. We shared a common experience and set of values. We felt privileged to be there and became a brotherhood that exists to this day, more than fifty years later.

Our underestimation of ourselves worked in our favor. We came with no expectations, a bunch of smart working-class kids who challenged each other in a spirit of friendly competition to achieve more than we ever knew we could. It was silent pressure, not overt or intentional, but there, nonetheless.

LESSONS MCBRIDE TAUGHT ME

Our teachers, eighty percent of whom were priests and brothers who committed themselves to the welfare and maturation of a group of boys, taught valuable lessons that remain with me to this day. There was math, history, science, English, and the other academics one would expect to learn at a high school. But of equal, if not greater value, were character-building lessons. They taught us:

Responsibility and Commitment

The faculty helped me and my classmates understand our responsibilities to our family, church, and community. "Real men understand their responsibilities and honor them," they said. We also learned that it was the duty of a man to keep his commitments. Our teachers hammered home to us that you don't commit to something without a willingness to give it your full measure. "If you can't honor your word, you're not worth much," was the mandate. "You're not a man; you're a boy."

To Be 'Good,' not 'Great'

We were taught the value of being "good" men, not "great" men. A focus on being good rather than great makes a better society because good men don't take their duties and responsibilities lightly. Greatness has its flaws. There are many casualties along the path of those who aspire to greatness instead of goodness. Goodness is getting involved with your community. It's living with purpose and serving others and providing opportunities to young people.

Opportunity was the great gift given to me at McBride, which opened my eyes to my potential and gave me visibility into what I could be and who I could become. I view it as my responsibility to pass that gift along to others.

Selflessness

The priests, all of whom had taken a vow of poverty, came to work every day in exchange for room and board. The example of their selflessness, putting up with the hijinks of fourteen-to-eighteen-year-olds, helped me understand what I could be. Otherwise, I would have ended up just another working-class kid from the mean streets of St. Louis. They gave freely of themselves, leaving a legacy of what serving other people is all about.

Living Your Faith

To the priests at McBride, Christ's message was straightforward: Love one another and do unto others as you would have them do unto you. They taught us that our faith requires us to find ways to help people and that bringing hope to someone or giving them a hand up doesn't require grand gestures.

Generosity

We were taught to be generous with what we had been given. For me, that legacy is expressed in providing financial support to ministries with underprivileged children.

I enjoy working with a Catholic Church program in St. Louis called Boys Hope Girls Hope. The program helps academically motivated middle and high school students rise above disadvantaged backgrounds and become successful in college and beyond. Our goal is to graduate young people physically, emotionally and academically prepared for post-secondary education and productive life, breaking the cycle of poverty, drug addiction, gang-life, and broken homes.

Another program my wife and I participate in focuses on educating the children of Bangladesh. More than one hundred sixty million people live in the country, twenty-five million who are ultra-poor — many of them children who are lucky to get one meal a day. The nation is also beset with illiteracy.

Children have to take an exam to get into the school system. If their parents can't read, however, the kids have no chance. That's why we helped start a two-year preschool program that prepares children to take the exam. My wife and I refer to them as "Sally schools" — a reference to my mother, whose education ended in the sixth grade.

For me, the reason was very personal, one born out of my time at McBride: I feel there is no greater tyranny than having an uneducated mind. I remember fondly the day a seventeen-year-old mother of one of the students said to me,

"I'm so happy my child will have a better opportunity than I did."

Currently, we sponsor thirty Sally schools. By the end of this semester, the schools will have graduated a total of seven thousand children, many of whom move onto higher education. We believe that if we can get enough children through to graduation, some will emerge as significant contributors to Bangladesh society and use reason rather than superstition and fear to lead the country toward a better future.

LESSONS FOR YOUNG MEN

All of the lessons I learned at McBride apply to any young man who desires to build his character and aptitude for success in life, but they are not the only ones. Here are others you can and should put into practice.

Have a positive mindset. Give someone a smile, a moment of uplift.

Get involved with community activities. Growing up, my sons were involved in a program in our parish that assisted the elderly. They would help older people get to church, or sit with them in their homes while their spouses ran errands or went to the doctor. They began coming home telling me about their experience with these seniors, listening to their stories, and learning from them. By participating in such programs, you will benefit from the same rewards.

Make your life interesting and fulfilling. You can make your life what you want — dull and dreary or interesting and fulfilling. Choose the latter.

Accept challenges. Seek out responsibility and challenge. Keep learning. Invest in yourself, not just spiritually but also intellectually, learning skills so that you can contribute more.

Have a vision. Have a vision for your life and develop the skills needed to see it fulfilled. As a young man, my dream was to run a business, and I spent the first twenty-five years of my career learning how. At times, I got so far underwater I didn't think I could kick my way to the surface. Still, I progressively sought more responsibility and challenge until I reached the level where I am now.

Find out who and what you want to be. You have to invest in yourself if you expect others to invest in you — spiritually, mentally, professionally, in the community, and so forth.

Go from "me" to "we." Human beings tend to be very "me-centric." Our society has transitioned from, "I'm here to serve a greater purpose" to, "how can I benefit me?" But a constant focus on "me" leaves you in a chronic state of unhappiness. If you can't get past me, you will never be successful in anything. Making and fulfilling your commitments is how you go from selfishness to selflessness, from "me" to "we."

CONCLUSION

The saying goes, "When God closes one door, he opens another." That's precisely what happened to me. I believe I was sent to McBride to realize my full potential. The relationships formed with my classmates there remain to this day.

Sadly, the school no longer exists. Its doors closed in 1971. Many of the students went to another Marianist school, Chaminade College Preparatory School, named after Blessed William Joseph Chaminade, a 17th-century French Catholic priest.

However, if I could write an epitaph for my time there, it would read: I would not be the man I am today had I not gone to McBride. They taught me how to be a man, just as they promised.

REVIEW QUESTIONS

1. How would you describe your high school experience?

2. Who were your biggest influences while in high school?

3. What lessons did you learn that you carry with you today?

CHAPTER THREE

ROOM 309

My first homeroom as a freshman at McBride was room number 309. It was more than a place to begin the day's activities; to refer to it in that manner is an injustice. Instead, Room 309 was a laboratory where creativity was sparked, lifelong friendships formed, and Christian morals and values ensconced. It was also an incubator of sorts. I entered the room as a boy and left on a clearly-charted course to become a man.

TOTAL STRANGERS TO LIFELONG FRIENDS

One of the milestone events in Room 309 that I remember fondly (there were many) was how quickly a group of strangers became lifelong friends.

When I entered McBride, I knew no one. I recall sitting at my desk the first day, and a student at the desk to my right introduced himself. "Hi, I'm Dan Wiese," he said, extending his hand in an offer of friendship. "Hi, I'm Joe Nettemeyer," I replied and shook his hand, accepting the offer.

That simple exchange was the start of a lifelong friendship, which is true of my relationships with many classmates. It was also the start of my efforts to meet people. I decided that if Dan was going to introduce himself to others, I would too.

As first-year students, we physically transitioned into manhood, a rite of passage fraught with wild emotional swings, changing voices, and the looming sense of not understanding what was taking place in our bodies. As a result, acceptance by friends was of paramount importance; rejection would have been emotionally crushing. I realized quickly that those concerns were completely unfounded.

Even though several of the students came from the same parishes and knew one another, there were no cliques or barriers to forming relationships. Many of us have now been friends for over fifty years, and it all started in Room 309 when one person extended his hand to shake mine.

Forming friendships is not the only reason Room 309 was special. We reported as the homeroom for group events, elected class representatives, and worked together to be part of our community. We also competed against each other without realizing it. That is what happens when you put a group of smart people together. We all try hard to keep up.

Room 309 was also like a boot camp of sorts. The Marianist priests and brothers began teaching us the required courses we were to take as freshmen—English composition, Latin, history, civics, algebra, and biology — and made sure we functioned as a unit. Spirit awards were given for different initiatives and programs that we as homerooms engaged in. The homeroom that did the best job won a banner that we would hang in the classroom acknowledging our accomplishments. Each morning at roll call, the teacher would recognize any student who had distinguished himself in some way, reinforcing the positive things we had done.

Everything in that room was structured to help us function as a group to affect positive change. The teachers helped us realize that if we stepped up, we could accomplish anything.

HIGH EXPECTATIONS IN LIFE AND WORK

Within the diocese of St. Louis, McBride had a reputation for having high expectations.

The priests and brothers had them, our parents had them, and we as students also had high expectations of each other.

That ethic led to me having high expectations in my personal life and career. As an adult, I see it as my responsibility to get the most out of people to discover what they are capable of. My children will attest to that. I pushed them to excel, not just cruise through life, and I do the same thing with my grandchildren and my nieces and nephews. They will tell you that conversations with me were like putting someone between a rock and a hard place — I would not give them room to waste time.

Having high expectations is also part of my role at Valin. Since becoming CEO, I have led the company to pay for fifteen of our employees to earn master's degrees. When they ask what my expectations are, I tell them, make straight "A's." Anything less is unacceptable — and they do!

I am also on the advisory board for the Texas A&M School of Industrial Engineering. In my lectures there, I often ask the audience, "What do you think my expectations ought to be as an employer? Someone who gives average effort or someone who gives their best?" I also challenge the students by asking, "Do you want to go through life and be the best C-student you can, or do you want to excel? Do you want to be a C-student in your marriage, as a parent, or in your profession? If not, then break the bad habits of mediocrity and satisfaction with average effort."

Why are my expectations so high? Because that's what I learned at McBride, and I see it as my responsibility to pass that on.

Having high expectations wasn't the only lesson I learned. Something else I picked up was the love of reading.

I was an insatiable reader as a child. My mom would tell me that if I found a piece of paper on the ground, I would pick it up and read both sides. I would check six books out of the library, read them in two weeks, and then check out six more. Such was my voracious appetite for reading.

At McBride, upperclassmen expanded my perspective on what I should be reading. To this day, I still exchange books and have discussions. My goal now is to read one book a week, and usually, I am on target.

Ten Dollar Tennis Shoes

As a thirteen-year-old freshman, I was 6'3" and was re-cruited to play basketball. (Actually, the coach came and told me I was *going* to play basketball.)

McBride was an Irish high school, and our colors were orange and green. As a basketball team, we emulated the Boston Celtics, who wore black Converse Allstars. Coming home one day, I told my dad I had made the team and need-ed a pair of these shoes. "The coach said we had to wear these shoes," I said.

My father took me to Famous-Barr, a downtown depart-ment store, and the salesman brought out the shoes and fit-ted them on my feet. I was excited because I was going to get my black Converse Allstars. Then, my father asked the price. "Ten dollars," the salesman said. At that time, ten dollars was a lot of money for tennis shoes, especially for my parents.

Dad instructed the salesman to wrap the shoes up and went to pay for them. I'll never forget that moment. He looked at me with a stunned expression and said, "I've never paid ten dollars for a pair of shoes in my life." But he did for me. Then he made sure I got a job so the next pair I had to pay for.

Fulfilling My Parents' Dream

Academically, math, history, and English composition were the courses I was passionate about — biology, not so much. But I did not want to bring home a bad grade, so I did what I had to do. And I wasn't the only one who knew that if we didn't give our best effort, we were letting our parents down.

Getting into McBride was a fulfillment of my parents' dreams. My mom's education ended in sixth grade and my dad's in eighth grade, so neither got to finish school. But their son had an opportunity, which they couldn't fully comprehend, and they wanted me to realize my full potential.

In study halls, students would tutor one another. We relied on each other to help us gain a greater understanding of the curriculum. We had to take two years of Latin, a dead language, but it was the church's language until Vatican II. After Latin, I took Spanish. While I wasn't excited about it, I knew I had to do it. The teachers taught us that to be a fuller individual, you have to gain some degree of mastery in these topics, and they pushed us to get the most out of the classes.

MY 'AH-HA' MOMENT

I was at McBride in the mid-60s. We had graduates from the 1940s and 50s who were very successful talk to us — educators, lawyers, judges, and businesspeople. Hearing them speak helped me focus on my life's goal: to run a business.

As a senior, I remember hearing that if you were in the top ten percent of income in the U.S., you made twenty-five thousand dollars per year. I was so confident I could run a successful business, I told a friend, "I'm going to make twenty-five thousand a year." When I graduated college, I worked for companies that taught me how to run a business and had high expectations. In those companies, I flourished. When challenged, I always excelled.

THE 'BOYS AT McBRIDE' BROTHERHOOD

The McBride faculty worked hard at creating an environment of brotherhood that exists to this day. We were placed in this "laboratory" where high expectations were put on us academically and morally, and where Christ's teachings were the standards that would take a group of confused, early adolescent boys and turn them into men.

These Marianist priests and brothers taught us that we had to transition in our faith from celebrating it to living it — and they did it for nothing more than service to God. They built the brotherhood by insisting we show each other respect. We helped classmates who were struggling, held student court, and enforced our code of conduct. These teachers and mentors engaged us in the pursuit of doing the right thing. They taught us the difference between being "me" focused and "we" focused.

We embraced that ethic and lived it. As such, our relationships have endured to this day. We take pride in our brotherhood. We seek to help one another whenever we can. We raise scholarship funds for young men to attend Chaminade, the Catholic school that took McBride's place after it closed so that others might have the same experience. To this day, we remain brothers committed to doing the right thing. That was the gift we received from our years at McBride.

McBride shaped the man I am today, and I will always be grateful to be one of the boys of McBride.

LESSONS FOR YOUNG MEN

When I reflect on the lessons learned in Room 309 and at McBride in general, these questions come to mind, which I would like to pass on to young men:

What are you doing to build a better community? There are multiple levels of that: your home, profession, and society at large. It does not require grand acts to move the world forward. The cumulative effect of little actions by a community of people can turn small ripples into a wave.

What's your journey of personal discovery? What are your goals? Who and what are you trying to be?

What have you done to alleviate another person's burden? In society, we think everything revolves around money, but that is not the case. A smile, a kind word and a prayer are gifts. When people are honestly and sincerely praying for you, it is the most personal of gifts. It's not about how much money, but rather the intangibles — the acts of human kindness—that build a better society.

REVIEW QUESTIONS

1. What is a favorite homeroom or high school memory?

2. How much did your parents' expectations influence your efforts to achieve scholastically?

3. What is one lesson you carry with you today that you learned from high school?

CHAPTER FOUR

MY BRIDE

A man's wife is the most important person in his life. That's certainly true for me. My wife Jane and I have been married for over forty-four years, and I can confidently say that she has made me a better man.

I met Jane through a blind date arranged by her cousin, a high school friend of mine. I helped him remodel an old house, and one day he mentioned his cousin and said he would like us to meet. I agreed, and he set us up.

When I arrived at Jane's parents' home, her identical twin met me at the door. Not having met Jane, I wasn't aware it *was* her twin. Then Jane appeared, she and her sister giggling at their good-natured sleight of hand, and invited me in. We sat down on the living room sofa, stared at each other for a few minutes in awkward silence, and then started talking.

We went to see a movie, then met some friends at a popular twenty-four-hour St. Louis breakfast restaurant, Uncle Bill's Pancake House, which is still in operation. She and I sat in the booth and talked until two-thirty in the morning. We discovered that despite our earlier discomfort, conversation was, for us, a relatively easy feat to accomplish. My biggest impression of that first date was how genuinely comfortable we were with each other. When we returned to her house, I asked her out again, and we started dating regularly. I had finished college, but Jane was in her third year of nursing school. So, often, our dates consisted of her studying while we spent time together.

I was blessed with a high IQ and could remember things easily, so getting A's was never a problem. It was different for Jane. But what she lacked in retention, she made up for with discipline and hard work, efforts that enabled her to master the subjects and make A's. That personal discipline was something I highly admired. After we married and had a family, she brought that structure to our children and taught them how to study.

Something else I admired, Jane always dressed respectfully and always in good taste. She never invited the wrong kind of attention. She conducted herself in a manner that engendered respect, an example she has set for our daughters throughout her life.

Speaking of respect, I never picked Jane up unless my car was clean. I would find ways to clean it even in the dead of winter. She was impressed that I thought enough of her to go to the trouble, but I did it as a sign of respect, that my time with her was important. The clean car was a visible clue.

One weekend, we drove to Hermann, a Missouri community populated with wineries and restaurants. Black-eyed Susans lined the roadside, so we stopped and picked some. The flowers were nice, but they were loaded with bugs, which got all over the back seat. She knew how picky I was about keeping the car clean and waited to see my reaction. Patiently, I said, "Let's stop and clean out the bugs." She told me years later that was when she knew I was hooked and serious about the relationship.

We had been dating for nearly a year by the end of 1975, and I knew she was the person I wanted to marry. We had been talking about marriage prospects and had even gone to a jeweler to look at rings. She showed me what she liked. It was expensive by my standards. I was near broke, but I wanted her to be my wife, so sometime later, I bought the ring, then picked her up at her dorm, drove about two blocks, stopped, and sitting in the front seat of the car, asked her to marry me. Today, couples stage these things, and I could have done that, but the moment was right, so I popped the question.

We drove to her parents' house, where I asked her father for his permission to marry Jane. He was sitting at the kitchen table paying bills. He looked up and said, "Sure, here are her dental bills." I reached out, took them, and said, "I'll take care of that." As awkward as that interaction was, it started a close relationship that lasted until his death. At his funeral, I gave the eulogy and thanked him for giving me the hand of his daughter.

We married eight months later, in January 1977, at her parish church. We were planning to get married that spring, but as part of the Boomer generation, many people were getting married at the time. We knew we had to get an opening on the church calendar.

Back then, couples were required to marry in the bride's parish. We tried to get the church and reception hall scheduled for the same day. We needed a large hall due to family size — both of us came from large families and expected many of our relatives to attend the wedding and reception. They gave us choices of late '77 or early '78, or we could get the church and a nice reception hall on January 29, 1977. We took it, much to her mother's displeasure. Jane's sister got married at the end of October, and ninety days later, we would walk the aisle. Jane said, "Mom will be upset about this." I replied, perhaps a bit too curtly, "She'll get over it."

My mom and dad insisted on paying for the catering and bar tab. In those days you could do a wedding for four thousand dollars. Today, fifty-thousand is the threshold. Four hundred eighty guests attended the wedding, seventy percent of whom consisted of family. The remainder were friends and people important to both our families. It was fourteen degrees outside on that January day. Jokingly, we called it an "arctic" wedding. But we didn't care; we were starting our lives together.

We honeymooned in a much warmer climate, Panama City, Florida — a friend let us use a condo he owned. I remember that was the first time Jane had seen a major body of water. We drove from Panama City to Orlando to visit Disney World. (Now, when people ask what we did on our honeymoon, we say we went to Disney World.)

We returned from the honeymoon a week later and went to work. We set a goal to buy a home and saved diligently to set aside enough money for a down payment. She and I always worked together to accomplish goals and objectives.

Jane was an intensive care nurse. She worked three weeks of days, and the fourth week worked nights, eleven to seven. She also had to work every other weekend. I was off on the weekends but picked up second jobs to accumulate enough savings to make the down payment on our first house, which we bought in the summer of 1978. Three months later, Jane came home and said, "I'm pregnant."

MANAGING MARITAL CONFLICT

That was a scary time because we suddenly had a mortgage, and soon, our first child would be born. It was manageable with my income and hers, and when she asked, "Can we do this?" I reassured her we could. Jane had to learn how to deal with uncertainty — there's always a degree of uncertainty in any marriage — but I was very confident. That was a bit of a rub, but she trusted me, and we worked through it.

There were no significant hurdles to get through during those early years. We focused on common goals and worked on those together. We were always at least ninety percent in agreement on most topics. Practically the only time Jane got upset with me was when she felt I was too hard on the kids. The way I looked at it, my job was getting them ready for life. The world would mistreat them, and they needed to know how to deal with it.

A part of my personality is I don't like being told what to do. If you tell me what to do, I'll mentally close the door and ignore you. Initially, Jane would get pressure from her mother to do certain things, and I would resist. I would say, "If your mother wants to pay for it, we'll do it; if not, we won't. It doesn't matter what she wants; it's what we want."

The Bible says, leave your father and mother and cleave to your husband. Jane grew less dependent on her parents and learned to depend on me. And when we moved out on our own, we learned to depend on each other — to be "one flesh."

Jane also changed her process to get buy-in from me. That's a vital key to a good marriage: adjust your approach to fit your partner. The most important lesson we learned early on was assessing the effort mutually and not criticizing the process. There's no one right way to do things (Unless you talk to my grandmother. To her, there was only one way to do something: her way.).

Marriage has to be a series of compromises. If Jane wanted something done this Saturday and I had planned to do something else, I would say, "Tell me what you want done, and I'll put it into my schedule." We had to learn how to get the other to buy-in. There were moments of stiff disagreement, but we would talk and figure it out.

In forty-four years, we had fewer than ten raised voice arguments, and seventy-five percent of those were in the first fifteen years of our marriage. We realized that wasn't productive and stopped doing it. I came to understand the kind of environment I needed to create for Jane to listen, and she learned what worked for me. You have to continue to grow in your understanding of one another if you want marriage to succeed.

QUALITIES IN A WIFE

I wanted to marry someone of my faith, who shared the same moral code, and who had an example of commitment from her parents. I didn't want a woman who would be dependent on me financially but who could take care of herself if something happened to me. I also wanted someone I felt passionate about, not just sexually but in a partnership way. Jane perfectly exemplified all those traits.

For Jane and me, the family was and is essential. We were both raised in the Catholic church, so we shared a common set of values, one of which was that you married for life. If you're getting married in the church, you're making vows before God and have to take them seriously as sacred. Her parents were married for sixty-nine years and mine for forty-two, so we had models to follow.

QUALITIES OF A GOOD HUSBAND

My father always said the best gift you can give your children is to love their mother. I feel more strongly about Jane today than I did when we first married. She is my life partner and has made me complete. We have tackled life's challenges together for forty-four years, faced them as a team, and never abandoned one another.

My motivation is the same now as it was then — love my wife, be a good husband, and provide opportunities for our children.

MARRIAGE AND SOCIETY

Family is the cornerstone of society, and marriage between a man and woman is the cornerstone of the family.

Marriage and family are divinely ordained institutions that strengthen a community, especially when married couples are committed to success. Marriage is about taking the responsibilities each partner has accepted and doing the best you can to live up to them. The family unit is the cornerstone of civilized society. If a couple is providing opportunity and working for their children's common good, society moves in the right direction.

I look at single-parent homes today with dismay. Instead of the man being the responsible party, the woman is forced to marry the government. The man is absent, having abdicated his responsibilities. Often, the children, looking for a sense of family, find it in gangs.

I am convinced the solutions don't lie in Washington, D.C. or state capitals. Answers are in the communities and institutions like family; problems can be solved at that level. A community prospers when children are nurtured in the structure of a family unit. Without a healthy family environment, we diminish as a community and nation.

MARRIAGE AND CHILDREN

The most important thing marriage can do is bring children into the world and nourish them in every respect: intellectually, physically, emotionally, and spiritually.

When our first child was born, I gained an entirely new sense of purpose in life. It made me raise my game because nothing would stand in my way of providing opportunity for my children.

I thought I understood love, but I didn't fully gain an appreciation of it until I held my child in my arms. I remember sitting in a chair next to my wife's bed in the hospital and said to her, "I promise you; I won't let you down."

It's also vital for parents to earn the respect of their children, to set high expectations, and challenge them. Suppose they see you and your spouse setting high expectations for yourselves, living a life you want them to emulate. In that case, they will likely grow up following your example.

MARRIAGE AND CAREER

Starting a family motivated me to get more serious about my career. I had been doing okay but knew I needed to improve, so I got into an executive MBA program.

Jane kept a very tight structure for the kids. She would put them to bed by seven and go to bed shortly after. I would study all night, and it wasn't unusual for me to fall asleep at my desk with a pile of books laid out in front of me. I still had to get up at six-thirty to do my job, however. Still, I was driven to complete the program, knowing it would enable me to do more for my family and give them the best opportunity I could.

COUNSELING YOUNG COUPLES

One of the rewards of being married for so long is that we get to conduct premarital counseling with young couples in our parish. Something we often encounter is that for them, the focus is on the wedding. But then I ask, "What about the next day?" I also ask the young man, "Is this the woman you want to raise a family with?"

We would also seek to learn if they were on the same page religiously, whether Christian or non-Christian. We would find out their views on handling money; it's one of the leading causes of divorce. I tell young men, "You can't be married to a materialistic woman; she will spend you into oblivion. Instead, spend your money on providing security and opportunity for your children. Each is a gift from God."

We also ask if they are someone you want to spend time with, stressing the importance of focused time with each other. You have to stay connected to your wife, and she has to be willing to do that as well.

Jane and I would always take time on the weekends for one another. We would put the kids to bed and just sit and talk. Now, Jane spends time with her parents for several weeks each summer, and I always look forward to her coming home. I'm happy when she returns because I enjoy being in her presence all the time.

CONCLUSION

I have spent almost forty-six years with Jane, including our courtship. Ours is not a perfect marriage, mind you, but we don't fight much or yell at each other. We prefer to invest our time enjoying each other's company instead.

We have discovered what constitutes a good marriage through the years: making a commitment and putting effort into building a life together. To that end, Jane and I have created a relationship characterized by abiding love, explicit trust, and deep commitment — and I never want to do anything that would violate that.

LESSONS FOR YOUNG MEN

My advice to young men falls into two categories: pre-marital and marital.

BEFORE MARRIAGE

Be on the same page spiritually. The Bible says not to be unequally yoked. If you're a practicing Christian, you want to marry a practicing Christian. You must be aligned where your faith is concerned. You will need a common, shared faith to fall back on in hard times. Faith is foundational to a good marriage.

Talk about practical matters. As important as it is to discuss spiritual matters, it is just as critical to talk about practical: money, lifestyle, sex, and so forth. You need to be aware of any red flags that arise. Unless you share values in all of these areas, you won't have a good marriage. Marriage isn't about fresh pastries every morning and a kiss on the cheek. Life comes with adversity, so you must have common faith and values.

Talk about money at length. You and your fiancée have to be on the same page regarding your spending habits. If one is a saver and the other isn't, you won't have a good marriage. In that environment, you will often be at odds with one another and stress over paying the bills, not always knowing how you will do that. Not being able to manage money indicates a lack of discipline. You will not have a good partnership if one or the other of you is undisciplined with your finances.

DURING MARRIAGE

If you start with shared faith, values, and commitment, you will have a foundation upon which to build a strong, healthy marriage. You become an example to your children and others — living Christ's message of love for one another.

Have integrity in your commitment to your spouse. Be honest and don't make false promises. Work together to accomplish the goals you have for the marriage, even if that sometimes means having difficult conversations.

Live the example. You can't ask your wife to do something you're not willing to do.

Be financially responsible. Live within your means. Marriage is not about material things but eternal.

Accept each other for who you are. Anyone who marries another person thinking they can change them is on a fool's errand. Typically, by the time a couple gets married, each party is set in their ways.

Be on the same page about parenting. One of you can't be strict and the other permissive. Children need to hear the same message from each parent. They need consistency and to know what their limits are.

Practice healthy communication. Communication is one of the big issues that couples struggle with. Healthy communication involves talking and listening, seeking to understand what motivates your partner.

Reassure your spouse of your commitment. There can be a sense of, "If I tell my partner this, they will abandon me." You can't have a constructive marriage if you're concerned about the other person's commitment or fear them walking out. You have to build assurance that you are committed to marital success. Do that through your actions, not just your words.

Show respect for your spouse. One of my concerns about society's current state in America is that people don't respect one another. The same thing is true in marriages. If you're disrespectful to your spouse, you won't have much of a relationship.

Never criticize your wife in front of someone else. If you have a beef with your wife, talk to her about it; don't go to friends and criticize. All you're doing is saying you made a wrong choice. Women have a mutual responsibility, but the man has to set the example. Start by doing the right thing for her. Disagreements are private; honor one another in public.

Marriage isn't about having a party and jumping between the sheets. It's about building a life together. Divorce is the easy way out; a good marriage requires work and commitment. And it starts with you, the man.

REVIEW QUESTIONS

1. Name a couple who, in your opinion, models a good marriage.

2. What qualities need to be present in a successful marriage?

3. What is the most important lesson you learned from this chapter?

4. What is something you learned that you didn't already know?

CHAPTER FIVE

STEADFAST IN THE FACE OF DEFEAT

They say the four most difficult disruptions a person can face are the birth of a child, a loved one's death, a job change, and relocation. Jane and I went through all of those in ten months.

My oldest son was born in February 1986, so we were adjusting to that dynamic. Then, in the fall of that year, my employer, Emerson Electric, offered me the Vice President of Sales and Marketing position in a forty-million-dollar division. It was the next step in advancing my career but would require us to relocate.

Jane and I were native St. Louisans from large extended families. It was a difficult, emotionally challenging decision, complicated by the fact my father was in the hospital suffering from heart issues.

After receiving the job offer, I went to my father's hospital room and told him his son had become a vice president. That lifted his spirits, and there was a look of joy on his face. I also said I was concerned about leaving him and Mom while he was in this condition. He looked me straight in the eye and said firmly, "Your mother and I have been taking care of ourselves for years. You have a responsibility to your family, and this will give you the opportunity you need." Fortunately, Dad's condition improved, and he was released from the hospital.

We moved to Atlanta and bought a house. The timing was such that we flew down on December 30 and closed the next day. We flew back to St. Louis, and within an hour of our return, we got a call that my parents had gone to a hotel for a New Year's Eve party. After he and Mom danced, Dad said he was feeling tired, sat at the table, and had a heart attack. They couldn't resuscitate him in time, and he suffered ninety percent brain damage as a result. He held on for four weeks.

In the meantime, we had to vacate our house in St. Louis, which we sold. A moving company packed up our things and, on January third, loaded the moving van and left for Atlanta. With my father seriously ill in the hospital, I felt helpless, as if I wasn't a good son. But, regardless, I had to go to Atlanta to unlock the house for the movers. Then, I flew straight back to St. Louis and, with my family, waited a week for the physician's assessment. The nurse ushered my mother, brother, and me into a small meeting room where the doctor explained what happened and how much brain damage my father had suffered. He told us there was little possibility he would survive. If he did, he would not be the man we knew. The doctor recommended that we take dad off of life support.

Once the physician laid out my father's condition, my mother and brother turned to me, the eldest son, to decide. It was a decision fraught with emotion. I felt almost like Christ when he asked God in the Garden of Gethsemane, "Can this cup pass me from me?" However, I knew my father would not want to live a life impaired in any way, so, reluctantly, I said yes.

The company I took over had been poorly managed for several years and had to be fixed. I drove back to Atlanta because my boss wanted it done in sixty days. When my father passed away, I went back for the funeral. Two days after the service, I received a memo from my boss telling me that we were not hitting the objectives — I had inherited them; it wasn't my plan — and that I wasn't doing my job. The pressure I felt during this emotionally-devastating time was enormous. Yet, I knew Dad would want me to live up to my commitments, so I returned to Atlanta and accepted the boss's mandate.

We did the turnaround, a feat for which I received a great deal of credit, although my boss and I had several heated arguments during that time. He had created an environment of uncertainly, more than once threatening me with the loss of my job. Were it not for my family, likely I would have told him to "pound sand" and either been fired or quit.

Later that year, in April, Jane said she was pregnant with our fourth child. She was overwhelmed because, unlike St. Louis, where we had lots of family, she had no support group in Atlanta. It was a real struggle. There were moments when I was hanging on by my fingertips, but I wasn't going to let go. If I allowed any of those things to beat me, I felt I would be letting both my family and father down — his legacy was my motivation.

The Ten Commandments come with a lot of "Thou shalt not," but one commandment says, "Honor thy father and thy mother." I wasn't going to dishonor my father by accepting defeat. The positive result was that I realized I had a greater capacity to deal with adversity than many people.

I got the job offer in October of 1986, and we moved to Atlanta on January 3, 1987. Four weeks later, my father died, twelve weeks later, our fourth child was on the way, and I was managing a turnaround in the business. It was a situation where I thought, "Is there anything else you want to throw at me?"

The lesson I learned is that hard times test a man's character. You have the instinct of fight or flight. It's easy to walk away from your responsibilities and much harder to stand your ground. It's a lesson I didn't learn suddenly. I persevered because I came from an extended family with a lot of grit who had instilled that in my generation.

In the movie *Apollo 13*, Ed Harris's character, Gene Kranz, the NASA flight director, said, "Failure is not an option." I was not going to fail. That would have been an abdication of responsibility to my family and my parents. The truth is, I felt there was nothing at which I could fail — I had to be successful at everything. I put a lot of pressure on myself to support my family and my mother who lived six-hundred miles away. I had a fourth mouth to feed. Business decisions were important — I couldn't give my boss a reason to ship me out — the stress of all that was huge.

Jane and I had been married ten years at that point. I knew that if I was going to provide opportunity for my children, I had to advance in my career. When Emerson offered you an opportunity for career advancement, you didn't turn it down because the next one wouldn't come. We were both in agreement with that. We knew we had to do this. It was part of our makeup as a couple and forged us into a tighter and tighter team.

When we moved to Atlanta, with three children and a fourth on the way, working was impossible for Jane. Thanks to my promotion, my salary covered our expenses, but we had to tighten our belts. Instead of lavish vacations every summer, we would pack the kids up and drive to St. Louis, where they and Jane would spend two weeks with family. I would fly out from there to go to other parts of the country for work. At the end of two weeks, we would load up and drive back to Atlanta. Those summer visits were good for our kids. They cemented relationships with their cousins that last to this day.

For Jane and myself, 1987 was a catalyst for growth. We gained confidence in each other that we could handle adversity and change. It prepared us for what I would go through years later during another tough year.

In 2019, I had a slight stroke and was diagnosed with a right carotid artery that was ninety-eight percent blocked. I had surgery the day before Thanksgiving. They stripped the artery clean and, fortunately, there was no permanent damage. I went back to work in 2020 — I was now CEO of Valin Corporation. We lived in Silicon Valley, California — and then the coronavirus pandemic hit. I questioned how we would run the company with everyone working from home. Still, we found it pretty easy with the technology and processes the management team used to enable communication.

During that time, I was exposed to someone Covid-19 positive and had to quarantine for fourteen days. Then, in September, I had major open-heart surgery and had to recover from that. But Jane and I were able to take it in stride because, in 1987, we learned how to cope with more adversity than some people get in a lifetime.

LESSONS FOR YOUNG MEN

Here are several key lessons that I learned regarding how to cope with adversity.

Break problems down into manageable steps. Don't let the size of the situation overwhelm you. Look at the problem and say, "I have to get from the first floor to the second." Figure out how to take each step, from one to the next, and put the problem into perspective. Break down your problems into actionable items.

I did that with the company I had taken over at Emerson. We had lost control of pricing, so we put pricing disciplines in place. The plant manager had overbuilt inventory, so I restructured our buy programs and leveraged our cost position, offering incentives to flush out the stock and convert it to capital. I also re-manned the sales organization, using the salespeople to grow our distribution network.

When I got there, the company was running thirty million in sales a year but losing six-hundred thousand. Three years later, when I left, we were doing fifty million in sales annually and making six and a half million in pretax profit.

At the end of 1990, another company wanted to buy the business. Initially, they had tried to buy it in 1986, offering sixteen million. In 1991, they paid forty-two million. The management team made the difference, but I was credited with fifty to sixty percent of the change, which led to career advancement within Emerson Electric.

Lean into your faith; it will carry you through hard times. Jane and I were in church every Sunday and got involved in parish activities. Our pastor checked in with me regularly to gauge my mental resilience, support that proved very helpful. I also believed that God doesn't give you a problem you can't handle. Find a way through challenges and discover growth in yourself and your faith.

On Sunday afternoons after services, I would sit down and ask myself, "What's the next thing I have to do?" God doesn't talk to you in a bombastic voice but comes in quiet inspiration. In those times of reflection, God came to me, not in direct communication but a "still, small voice." I would see or hear something and have an "aha" moment. God was very subtle, influencing me to do the right thing and take the next step.

Be willing to make tough decisions. Some of those steps involve making tough decisions. In business, that means making sure the company survives. You have no choice but to make difficult decisions, and sometimes that includes laying people off (which, for me, was the hardest decision I ever had to make). But you have to persevere through that. You either let problems break you or make you.

Refuse to cut and run. I refused to let adversity break me or to cut and run. That's character-shaping even when it's hard. Don't give in to failure and never run from a decision. We all want someone else to make the painful choices. You must make them and deal with the consequences, even if they are unpopular.

Express gratitude to God. My great-uncle was a Catholic priest, and he told me the simplest, most elegant prayer: "Thank you, God, for giving me the opportunity to serve you." I've been saying that every morning for fifty-five years. It's a moment of pause and reflection just to say thanks.

Use your mind. God gave you the ability to reason and solve problems. You can either throw up your hands or find out what God has made you capable of.

In 1987, I began to learn what God made me capable of. That year brought darkness into my life, but I learned to push back against it. That's where faith comes in. Christ gives us hope, but we have to live by His guidance. Triumphing over darkness and evil isn't easy, but you can't let it consume you.

REVIEW QUESTIONS

1. Describe a time in your life when you faced difficulty. How did you deal with it?

2. How important is the role of family during hard times?

3. What is one lesson you learned that you could teach others?

CHAPTER SIX

MY VOCATION AND DUTY

When God gives you an opportunity, take responsibility and move forward with duty and honor.

Opportunities always came to me in inflection points. The first was when Emerson offered me the Vice President of Sales and Marketing position for a smaller division. It required Jane and me to relocate to Atlanta. We were native St. Louisans with large extended families and thought we would never leave the area. But I knew if I didn't take the job, another opportunity might not come along. That was Emerson's corporate culture at the time.

That job challenged me and made me grow. It escalated my career that led to increasing responsibility but required more transfers, first to Indianapolis and then Pittsburgh.

After nine years in Pittsburgh, I reached a point where I felt I couldn't learn any more at Emerson. The company prepared me to do a bigger job, and I was confident I could run a business. Emerson would offer me that opportunity, but it would mean going to someplace off the beaten path, and I wasn't sure my bride was willing to live in a small town.

Taking the Reins at Valin

About that time, another inflection point occurred in the form of an unexpected opportunity to take over as CEO of Valin Corporation, a distributor and manufacturer serving the semiconductor industry, located in Silicon Valley. It was a big departure from what we were used to. As native mid-westerners, we were hesitant to make the leap to California. Still, I knew it would be the opportunity for me to grow something and be the driver. Jane agreed, so at the end of June 2001, we packed up and headed west.

After our arrival, an unwelcome inflection point happened: the dot com crash. I didn't realize the impact the crash was going to have on equipment manufacturers. Before that, if you could write a business plan, you could get twenty-five million dollars in seed funding. But when things went down, they went down hard. Our company's revenue dropped from seventy-five million to twenty-five million in four months, so I accepted a twenty-five percent pay cut. We had taken on the biggest mortgage of our life, but the salary reduction was necessary to keep the business operating.

Two thousand one was a tough year. The dot com crash started the year in a downward trend, 9-11 turned into a disaster, and Valin's revenues declined sixty-five percent in a six-month period. But we got through it. My twenty-one-year career at Emerson had prepared me to handle down cycles. I was confident I could get the business back on track. I knew what to do and was willing to make tough decisions.

I had moved from a major corporation whose whole focus was on making a profit quarter by quarter. Emerson had forty-one years of increased earnings and profits. The stock kept rising and was seen as a safe investment. But you made a lot of decisions in that environment that equated to living in the moment. I always felt frustrated that I had to sacrifice long-term growth plans I made at the altar of short-term profit.

That was probably the primary catalyst that drove me to accept the position at Valin. That, and the desire to take on a business and see it grow, even if it meant moving out of our comfort zone to Silicon Valley. I knew that if I could manage the downside, I could be much more successful on the upside.

We came out of the difficult period with a head of steam. We built the business up to one-hundred-sixty million in revenue, weathered the 2008-09 financial crisis, and acquired more than forty smaller distributors, which increased our customer base.

I was always confident I could fix whatever problems I faced — and I did. That confidence was built on decades of experience in dealing with challenges. At Emerson, I operated with a lot of cash on hand. The shift to being privately-owned carried a real danger of running out of money. However, I knew if I were successful, there would be greater rewards than a paycheck and bonus — there would be ownership.

PUTTING VALIN UNDER
EMPLOYEE CONTROL

Valin started as an ESOP (Employee Stock Ownership Plan) in 1988, with employees having thirty percent of the shares. When I came on board in 2001, we restructured the ESOP so employees would own seventy percent of the shares, and I would own thirty. I was the only remaining private shareholder. We were in that state until, in 2007, I structured a buyout of my shares, which made the company one hundred percent employee-owned.

I took that step because I felt people should share in the value they helped create. We have many good, hard working people, and my goal has always been to keep them employed. As CEO, I was running the business for the employee-owners.

I structured the deal over ten years so there would never be a cash flow issue. Whenever I felt the company needed to be cash positive, I would suspend payments. My objective was always to keep the company in a healthy financial position and never jeopardize it. Whenever I found myself in shallow water with my depth of experience, I sought out advisors who could help. You can't be an expert at everything, so surround yourself with people who can augment your skills and enhance your decision-making ability.

Duty and Honor to Family and Business

Duty is something that comes with the responsibilities for which you sign up. I have a duty to my wife and children — and my parents when they were living. When I have accepted responsibility, I must fulfill the duties that are included. That conviction was a trait passed down from my father.

My Duty to Family

My father had a cousin who was in poor health and had to go to a nursing home as she could not live independently. She asked Dad to help her sell her house, accumulate her investments, and manage her finances. He did that until her death.

Her only son was killed in a boating accident. He left a wife and three children. My father's cousin's will stated that whatever remained of her estate was to be divided into four equal parts: twenty-five percent to each of the grandchildren and twenty-five percent to my father for taking care of her estate.

She passed away a week before my father had his fatal heart attack. The attorney's office handling my dad's cousin's estate had also written my parents' will. I went to see him after my father passed away. He told us the changes to the cousin's will had never been filed, and the inheritance was solely in my father's name. We could choose not to file it, and my mother could have all the money. I knew that wasn't what dad would do, so I told the attorney to honor the will. My mother could have used the money, but that wasn't the right thing to do.

One of the Ten Commandments says to honor your father and mother. In that case, I honored my father. He taught me always to do the right thing. There is a lot of temptation when it comes to money. Still, I never wanted to do anything that would have incurred his disappointment.

MY DUTY TO VALIN

I always worked hard to give people a fair deal. My mom and dad were blue-collar, working-class people, and I grew up listening to them talk about what was good and bad in their bosses and the decisions they made. Today, when I ponder a decision, I ask myself what Mom and Dad would think about it.

I believe the average American worker has gotten a raw deal in the past thirty years, which is why I went to one-hundred percent ESOP at Valin. Mom and Dad would have appreciated it.

Business leadership these days is often driven by greed. Leaders make decisions that put people out of work, and I think that's wrong, especially when it's in the name of making short-term gains.

As an example, one California-based hardware store chain was acquired by a big-box home improvement retailer. The company was well-run and profitable, which made it an attractive acquisition prospect. The big-box company's board had committed a significant investment to upgrade the stores and give them a new look. However, the retailer had a new CEO who, instead of remodeling the stores, rescinded the board's decision and closed them, putting hundreds of employees out of work all in the interest of short-term gain.

I also remember actions taken by Jeff Immelt, former General Electric CEO, who, in 2010, received a government advisory committee position tasked to create jobs in the U.S. Instead, he decided to send the manufacture of MRI machines to China. These were high-tech devices, requiring specialized skills, so there was no need to ship the manufacture to a low-cost offshore producer.

These examples illustrate that, in many cases, the moral compass in business in this country is no longer there. These days, it is all about making a lot of money fast. But to do that means crushing people's welfare and putting their future at risk.

Keeping a business healthy and growing takes a long-term vision. When that turns into making short-term gains and increasing your stock price every ninety days, you lose sight of what is needed to be viable in five-to-ten years. You have to sacrifice the short-term to do that.

My approach is that you only have a healthy society if people have jobs and hope. A CEO has to create more than just quarterly profit but an environment of hope and opportunity. Since joining Valin, we have paid out over thirty-five million dollars to employees who are eligible to cash in their ESOP shares. I hope that Mom and Dad would be proud.

LESSONS FOR YOUNG MEN

Don't get enamored with the paycheck; take a job for growth. Look at what a job will do for you personally and professionally. Far too many people jump on a job because of money. But the long-term economic well being comes from getting a consistent paycheck, not necessarily more. You get more because you grow personally and professionally.

Too many people behind the curve on paying their bills take a job to get an extra five-thousand dollars. But you have to start all over and bring your A-game. If you don't prove yourself, you're gone, and then you're out of a job for the six months it takes to find another one.

Be willing to go the extra mile. When I look at joining a company, I ask myself, "Is this company willing to invest in me? Then, reciprocally, I ask, am I willing to invest the effort to take advantage of that? Am I willing to put in two extra hours of the week to grow personally and professionally?" Those have always been my hidden questions.

At Valin, I tell prospective employees, "We're willing to invest in you to upgrade your professional skills." But then I ask, "Are you willing to personally invest two hours of your time this week in doing that?" So many say, "No. You have to pay me to do that." You have to ask yourself the same question: Are you willing to go the extra mile to improve yourself?

Get up and answer the bell every day. I had greater responsibilities when I had a family. I had to give the full measure to have the income to provide shelter and opportunity to my family. That meant getting up every day, going to work, and putting in my best effort.

My grandparents and parents instilled in me a strong work ethic — if you don't work, you don't eat. God was reaching out to me in setting expectations. As I got out from underneath my parents' influence, I wrestled with my humanness: "I want to get maximum output with minimum effort." But that's an oxymoron.

Think long-term, not short-term gain. I am concerned that today, people sacrifice long-term wealth for the now. That happened in our company with employees wanting to borrow against their ESOP funds. We would have to counsel them that the funds were for their retirement, not to spend now.

There are two types of spenders: status and safety. Status spenders want to drive the expensive automobile. Safety spenders are always putting something away for rainy days — and there will be rainy days.

REVIEW QUESTIONS

1. Name a time when you had a growth opportunity. How did you respond?

2. What is your view of the responsibility of employers to their employees?

3. What do the terms "duty and honor" mean to you? How do they apply personally and professionally?

CHAPTER SEVEN

FOR OTHERS

"What does it profit, my brethren, if someone says he has faith but does not have works? Can faith save him? If a brother or sister is naked and destitute of daily food, and one of you says to them, 'Depart in peace, be warmed and filled,' but you do not give them the things which are needed for the body, what does it profit? Thus, also faith by itself, if it does not have works, is dead." James 2:15-17

A Catholic priest who was one of my McBride teachers went to Bangladesh in the late 1980s because he felt called to work with the ultra-poor. He started an NGO called the Poverty Eradication Program (PEP)[1].

Not long after, a group began in the U.S. — Partners in Sustainable Development International[2] — to raise funds for the various PEP initiatives. I was on the board for several years and served as chairman for a few of them.

---

1   http://www.pep-bd.org/
2   https://www.psdintl.org/

PEP has multiple programs: They buy land to set up small farms, help other people start small businesses, and work with other programs to get livestock. Their goal is to help the people of Bangladesh become self-sufficient. Their work doesn't stop there. They also dig deep wells to give people fresh, safe water, install waste disposal systems in small villages, and build dikes to prevent flooding and control water to make lakes and ponds for fishing to enable people to provide for their families.

The Bangladesh population consists of one hundred sixty million people living in a geographic footprint the size of Illinois. The population density is enormous, and much of the landmass is delta, prone to floods when the Himalayan snow melts.

Fifteen percent of the population lives in hard-core poverty and are lucky to get one meal a day. Not only do the people suffer from extreme poverty but also acute illiteracy. To get into the school system, however, the children have to pass a test, which means they must read.

In response to this need, PEP started kindergarten and first-grade programs, not unlike the Head Start programs in the U.S., to provide children with early-stage education, including the ability to read. The effort was successful but suffered from uneven funding. There may be sixty schools one year and twenty-five the next.

SALLY'S SCHOOLS

I sit with my grandchildren, read books, and teach them their alphabet and numbers. We give them a working knowledge of the basics to prepare them for school. I looked at these Bangladeshi children like my grandchildren and wanted to provide them with the same opportunity.

Because we believe there is no greater cruelty in life than illiteracy, Jane and I committed to providing ongoing financial support. We sponsor thirty schools per year, about one thousand children, to get them ready to take the entrance test. It costs almost two thousand dollars per school, but we have funded it consistently because we didn't want children to go to school one year and not the next. Through another PEP program, we pay for children's uniforms to go to school once they graduate.

We do this for two reasons. First, if you don't give people hope, desperation is a seed of destruction. Second, this is something my mom, Sally, would approve of.

Mom's education ended in the sixth grade. Work on the farm was deemed more important. She always regretted not getting an education but wanted it for her children. My wife and I feel we were beneficiaries of my mom's desire for us to get an education and have done well personally and professionally as a result. For that reason, we call the schools we sponsor "Sally's schools" to honor her memory.

The good news is that the schools are succeeding. About ninety-eight percent of the students pass the test. (Unfortunately, because the country's death rate is so high, one percent of the students die from illness before finishing.)

GODLY GENEROSITY

I believe it is incumbent on us to find ways to help the least among us and to give them a hand up, not a handout. Look at the example of Christ. He took all of the world's sins on his shoulder and let himself be defiled and nailed to the cross so that we can have the opportunity for eternal life. He gave us free will; we still have a choice. But He said, "You can follow my path or choose your own. My path leads to eternal life."

That was a great act of love, and love requires generosity. You must have a generous heart, absorb the tough moments, and recognize those you love are human beings and will fail from time-to-time. You have to let them choose their path, understanding some will choose wisely and some, poorly.

I see Christ's example as an overarching sense of what I have to do to be a good follower. He put forgiveness into our faculty. Before Christ, the world was cold, brutal, and cruel. But he gave us hope that life could have a better outcome.

For me, that outcome includes having a generous heart. I have to put the slights aside, focus on the goodness in people, and build my life around others who have generous hearts. You're not going to have success with a selfish person.

That's where godliness comes in. A quote attributed to St. Francis of Assisi says we must preach the gospel every day and use words where necessary. Live and set an example of generosity if you want to be a leader. If you set a selfish example, people won't follow you.

THREE TYPES OF PEOPLE

I classify people into three buckets: contributors, takers, and those who need to be taken care of — children, the elderly, and the sick. I don't waste time on takers.

You can choose to be a contributor or taker, but a healthy person is a contributor in the sense of their well-being. When

I was dating different young women, I was looking for a contributor. My wife was a nurse and wanted to contribute that way. If you're going to be healthy, build your life around contributors, not takers.

We all contribute in different ways. Most people think it's related to giving money, but there are also activities. My parents didn't have a lot of money, but Dad was involved with the St. Vincent de Paul Society and, as a World War II vet, worked with the Veterans of Foreign Wars.

After he retired, he would go to the VA hospital in St. Louis three mornings a week and sit with the patients there; they would talk and play cards. When I asked why, he told me he served with them in the war and felt an obligation to give them a bright spot in their day. My parents were also active in the parish and worked to secure the funds to keep it operating. They held their responsibilities to my grandmother, too, helping on the farm.

That's not all my parents did to express their generosity. They included people in family events who had no family. One couple became surrogate grandparents because they participated in every event — holidays, weddings, and baptisms. Dad would bring people who had no family home to share Christmas dinner. "No one should spend Christmas alone," he said. And it was fun to have them. They enjoyed being there. I was always interested in their stories about their families and how they grew up.

I used to speak on behalf of Catholic Charities and would close my speech with this phrase: "We come to church on Sundays to celebrate our faith. Now we have to go out and live our faith. That means giving hope to people who need help."

In James, chapter two, verse seventeen, the Bible says, "Faith without works is dead." My parents' lives illustrated the meaning and intent of that verse. They lived their faith through countless generous acts, giving people in need hope and moments of joy. Their example has been my inspiration to live a life of generosity for others, and I would highly recommend you follow it as well.

LESSONS FOR YOUNG MEN

Spend your time with contributors. Spending your time with takers will thwart your personal growth. Their focus is on minimum effort, working the system, and blaming others for their problems. Being poor in spirit is much worse than being poor financially.

Don't define your life with average effort. Average effort produces average results. There could be no worse epitaph than, "Here lies the best C-student of life!" Committed Father, Committed Husband, Committed Professional are the results that a contributor mindset produces.

Remember Christ's sacrifice. Eternal life will be determined by your Christian commitment and efforts. It is not membership in an institution. It is about living a sacramental life.

REVIEW QUESTIONS

1. Name a time when you gave to someone in need. What were the circumstances? How did you respond?

2. What influences did you have in your life that pointed to the need for generosity?

3. If you could put Christ's example of generosity into words, what would you say?

CHAPTER EIGHT

FROM 'ME' TO 'WE'

The key to a powerful life is to change your heart to focus on others more than yourself.

THE COIN

Conrad Nettemeyer was my father's younger brother, my uncle, and my godfather. He was also an alcoholic.

He began drinking heavily in his younger years. It got so bad that by seven in the evening, he was a falling-down drunk. He would drink as many as twelve beers at lunch but had built up such tolerance that he could handle it — until he couldn't. It was difficult watching him self-destruct.

He lived in Roanoke, Virginia, and worked for Norfolk & Southern Railroad. There was a lot of alcoholism in their company. But his CEO, a recovering alcoholic, started a program where employees who had trouble with alcoholism could go into rehabilitation.

The company finally gave my uncle an ultimatum: Go to rehab or be out of a job. So, he went to an inpatient facility in North Carolina. He completed the program and was sober for the remainder of his life, twenty-six years. He died at age eighty. He regularly attended Alcoholics Anonymous meetings throughout his life because he had to fight the urge to drink every day.

My uncle was in his fifties when he went to rehab. I was thirty-five at the time. Knowing he was coming out of a long period of alcoholism, we hoped for the best. But like my father, as one of the men of the family, I needed to provide support. He needed to know he had his older brother's approval and that of his nephews and me as his godson. We had to be his cheering section, and we were.

I was concerned that he would backslide, but as the years passed, my admiration grew because he controlled that demon — not an easy task. I have seen both those who stay sober and many who slide back. Those who stayed sober were courageous. They had to face what led them down that road to begin with.

My uncle was buried in Roanoke, and I was asked to speak at the funeral on behalf of the family. I focused on the fact he always showed me unconditional love, which I felt was his legacy. As a token, his wife, my aunt, gave me his first-year sobriety coin. I carry it with me all the time. Those last twenty-six years took courage and faith. He put God first, and I have that coin, one of my most treasured possessions, as a testament to his fortitude and that it's possible to overcome any problem. If you can beat alcoholism, you can conquer anything.

FROM 'ME' TO 'WE'

The encounter with my uncle opened my eyes to my greater responsibilities — that life was more than just about "me" but "we" — and I began expanding the "we" philosophy to my extended family.

I want to believe that when my uncle saw his family's non-judgmental acceptance — especially that of my father, brother, and me — it buoyed him, enabling him to stay on the path to lifelong sobriety. One of his sons had the same problem. We got him into a program, and he has been sober for ten years. He also needed that support, and we gave it.

I began to examine how I could make a difference beyond my family's scope to the world. I had no large sums of money then, so I had to do it through my actions.

In 1993, while in Pittsburgh, I joined the Family Links board, an organization that provides shelters for battered women, family support, and education and counseling for children with developmental difficulties. I raised money as part of my board responsibility but volunteered in other ways as well.

When we moved to California, I got involved in the Partners in Sustainable Development board to support Bangladesh's educational efforts. I've been on the board of directors for the Children's Discovery Museum of San Jose to raise funds to support educators who could reach the Hispanic community. I also funded an outdoor park for use in teaching kids. I named it "Jane's Classroom" because I admired my wife's discipline and structure in teaching our children when they were young.

In recent years, I became involved with my alumni association to raise funds to help young men going to Chaminade, legacies of McBride graduates, to get scholarships. School has gotten much more expensive since I was at McBride.

Jane and I commissioned a sculpture, Christ the Teacher, which sits at the Chaminade campus center, now a green space called McBride Green. That triggered a lot of giving to the scholarship program.

I desire to provide young men and women with a moral compass, not just professional skills. You have to give back — go from "me" to "we" — that's a vital issue for me. I feel that is my responsibility and duty.

MAKING THE SHIFT FROM 'ME' TO 'WE'

We live in an environment of casual commitment. Shifting from "me" to "we" means that we adopt a higher standard, one where men and women accept responsibilities and live out their commitments to family, church, work, community, and society at large. It means going from talking a good game to living a generous lifestyle focused on others' welfare.

'ME TO WE' IN MY FAMILY

Living a "me to we" lifestyle meant being engaged in my children's activities. I was good at sports and made time to coach their soccer and baseball teams. I traveled a lot, so I managed my schedule to be in town for practices and spend the weekends watching them play. My family got one hundred percent of my attention on weekends. I wanted them to know that Dad would come and be focused, not distracted.

Every year, I would assess each child on the team and figure out how to teach them to improve their skills and knowledge of the game. Seeing children accomplish more than they thought possible was gratifying.

It also meant being a good son, doing what I could to take care of my parents and provide for their needs. I never wanted to do anything that would embarrass my mother and father, which meant selfishness couldn't be part of my agenda. They taught me to "do the right thing," a mantra that's woven into my life like a strand of DNA.

'ME' TO 'WE' IN THE WORLD

As my children got older, I found other ways to live out the "me to we" philosophy.

In my church, I raised funds to support parish ministries and missions. In business, I got involved with the National Association of Wholesale Distributors and, for eight years, was on the board for the Institute for Distribution Excellence, an educational arm of the association. I was chairman for five of those years and set records for research and book publications we sold to members and which became part of the Texas A&M School of Industrial Distribution.

I was invited to join the School of Industrial Distribution advisory board and have served there for seven years. They are in the process of constructing the campus building. Jane and I have contributed a significant amount of money to the project. In return for our efforts, the school will name a classroom after us. It is to be called "The Joe and Jane Nettemeyer Innovation Center."

I also guest lecture there several times a year, talking to students about how to develop business strategy. "Me to We" is also why I restructured Valin as one hundred percent employee-owned. I wanted our employees to share in the value they helped create.

Over time, I began focusing on providing opportunities for children. That's why Jane and I got involved with teaching Bangladeshi children how to read. It's why I joined the Children's Discovery Museum board and participate in other initiatives related to fostering underserved children's well-being.

Genuine accomplishment comes from making a difference in another person's life, and there are many ways to do it. It's not about grand gestures, either. Small acts can be just as impactful. Refocusing your values from "me" to "we" is how you get there. The following advice can help.

LESSONS FOR YOUNG MEN

Examine your heart. Change starts with the heart. That will influence your thought processes and help you overcome a "what's in it for me" mentality.

Get past selfishness. If you do, your rewards will be much greater. If you're myopically focused on your self-interests, you will get nowhere. Aspire to serve the greater good.

Look around your community. You will find many people with great need deserving of help. Then ask yourself how you can make a difference.

Give of yourself, not just your money. It's easy to write a check and then go your merry way, but the real "me to we" test is when you become involved with others by giving your time and talents. It's not money that determines the impact you have on life; it's the effort.

Take the long view. When I was young, only thirty-five percent of the population got a college degree. Most people started working right out of high school. I remember individuals laughing at me. They were making more money working union jobs than I was as a college graduate. But they weren't looking at the long haul. They had peaked at the job they were in; I was just beginning and was going to peak in my forties and fifties. The lesson: look beyond today to the future.

Make "Me to We" a lifestyle ambition. The great reward of having a generous heart is seeing people lift themselves up, moving from an "I can't" to an "I can" mindset. Selflessness is a true mark of manhood. Make living a selfless lifestyle your goal.

REVIEW QUESTIONS

1. What gift has someone given you that you cherish?

2. What difference can shifting from a "me-centered" to "we-centered" attitude make in your life?

3. What is one action you can take today to meet someone else's need?

CHAPTER NINE

'ME TO WE' MOMENTS

I have shared my story throughout this book. However, this chapter shines the light on several people who embraced the "me to we" philosophy, living it out through their God-given priorities of faith, family, duty, honor, community, and growth. Here are their stories, as told from my perspective.

FAITH

I have a good friend who was raised Catholic and drifted away. About twenty-eight years ago, he and I were having a conversation about faith. He hadn't been going to church. We had a lot of discussions, and he decided to go back.

He is in his eighties now and very active in parish activities, serving as an usher, project manager for a church remodeling plan, and fundraiser helping families afford Catholic school. He visits the elderly and infirm to serve communion and spend time with them. He follows up several times a week by phone to check on their welfare.

He was at a retreat years ago, and someone asked him who brought God into his life. He thought about it and replied, "Joe Nettemeyer. He challenged me to think about what my faith could be."

He came back to his faith with the resolve to make a difference and gives of himself unselfishly. He is a living example of the "me to we" philosophy.

FAMILY

My father-in-law passed away in 2020. Since then, I have spent a lot of time reflecting on his life. In 1951, he made a commitment to love his wife and kept it for sixty-nine years. They raised seven children on one income. I once told him, "You are the one man I know who can squeeze a nickel into a quarter."

He did his best for his family. They never lacked medical care, never went to bed cold, and were never hungry. He stepped up every day and delivered for the best interest of his family.

He was also very active in his parish, serving as an usher. He worked in the parish until the last eighteen months of his life. He lost his hearing and could no longer fulfill his responsibilities but attended every Sunday until his death.

DUTY

My wife's grandfather is an example of duty to his country, faith, and family. He was a World War I veteran. When the Armistice was signed, he was among a group of troops the Army moved to Belgium to occupy German positions and enforce the surrender. While there, he contracted pneumonia and was put in a field hospital.

The physician would come in every afternoon to examine the patients. He instructed the nurses to bathe and give a new gown to those he thought wouldn't survive the night. It would become their burial garment.

Jane's grandfather overheard the physician give those instructions on Christmas Eve. He also knew there was a Catholic church about a mile from the hospital. He got up, dressed in his uniform, and walked to the church to attend midnight mass. There, he prayed and committed his life to serve God. He then walked back to the hospital. A physician asked him to take off his uniform and put on the hospital gown, but he refused. He said he wasn't going to lay down and die.

He got through that ordeal, came home, and married a woman he was dating before the war. They had four children together. However, his wife had heart problems and died at age forty-two. He never remarried but chose to raise the children by himself.

Her grandfather never turned bitter despite his adversity. He attended mass every day throughout his life. He had a deep faith, believing that God intervened for him, helping him survive pneumonia, and he set that goal for us every day. His stern demeanor was betrayed by his faith-filled heart. He focused on his faith and his family. He was one of the most outstanding men I ever met.

HONOR

Throughout this book, I have talked about my father and the example he set, but he is the first person who comes to mind when I think about honor.

People trusted my father, often asking him to take on some responsibility that usually involved money because they knew he would never cheat them. His cousin, the woman I referred to in an earlier chapter, was one such example. She had fallen into poor health and had to live in a nursing home. She gave my dad power of attorney and entrusted him with managing her finances. He was a careful steward and never let the funds get frivolously spent.

In another instance, my maternal grandmother's nine children were clashing over control of her funds. The way my grandmother dealt with it was to make my father the executor of her estate. After her death, my dad made sure each of the children got an equal share.

Lastly, whenever an organization had some issue with money, they would ask my father to take the reins and straighten things out. That was the kind of integrity he had.

COMMUNITY

These two individuals have contributed more to the development of their respective communities than just about anyone I know. They are true ambassadors of the "me to we" philosophy.

Jan Wacker, Boys Hope Girls Hope

Jan Wacker personifies "me to we" by the way she lives.

She is the development director and driving force behind the Boys Hope Girls Hope program in St. Louis. Jan is making a big difference in the lives of young people who would otherwise have no hope apart from the program.

Monsignor John G. Sandersfeld

Monsignor Sandersfeld was the pastor of my parish when we came to California twenty years ago. He was a leader who helped parishioners start ministries that expanded our commitment to our community.

He lived a life of gratitude, especially for the parish members. In recalling his years in ministry, he once said, "I really thought about the people who formed my life and had an influence, and I want to express my gratitude to them. The people of the Church have made my life a life of joy, happiness, and fulfillment. It has always been a privilege to be a minister."

GROWTH

Father Ralph Siefert, the current president of Chaminade and a fellow St. Louisan, is the person who first comes to mind when I think about growth. The school's motto is Esto Vir, which is Latin for "be a man." The school's mission is to grow the complete man. Father Siefert has devoted his entire career to creating an educational environment where young men can develop their professional skills and a moral compass to live out their faith in society.

EPILOGUE

Fifty years ago, my father gave me a plaque with the following quote from President Theodore Roosevelt that has stayed on my wall to this day:

> *"It is not the critic who counts; not the man who points out how the strong man stumbles, or where the doer of deeds could have done them better. The credit belongs to the man who is actually in the arena, whose face is marred by dust and sweat and blood; who strives valiantly; . . . who at best knows in the end the triumph of high achievement, and who at worst, if he fails, at least fails while daring greatly."*

That quote reminds me to never undertake anything in my life without wanting to give total commitment. Life's challenges can be daunting. There is a great deal of advice out there given by those who choose to be academics versus practitioners. The practitioners have to make things happen;

they have to translate theory into action; they can ill-afford to be timid.

DARE TO BE TRIUMPHANT!
ESTO VIR - BE A MAN!

ACKNOWLEDGMENTS

The writing of *Esto Vir, Be A Man*, was inspired by the motto of Chaminade Preparatory High School, a Marianist high school in St. Louis, Missouri. The slogan embodies the mission of the school: to take boys and turn them into men. The educational environment provides young men with the technical skills necessary to be productive in life. More importantly, it develops the moral compass that gives them direction in living a life of contribution.

That same winning formula was also applied to the boys of McBride High School, a Marianist school I attended from 1965 to 1969. The young men who graduate from Marianist high schools may not always do the right thing, but they definitely know the right thing to do.

Today, doing the right thing is subject to broad interpretation fraught with conflicting messages, competing agendas and lowered expectations for young men. We live in a time where clarity is gained through the simplicity of message and focus on doing the right thing. I give personal thanks to the Marianist community that gave so much to me and other boys who were students at their high schools throughout the United States.

I would like to thank my friend Dirk Beveridge, who encouraged me to write this book and introduced me to the Throne Publishing team: Jeremy Brown, Tim Jacobs, Paul Chaney, Heidi Caperton, Kendra Paulton, Earl Menchhofer, and Vicki Rich. They helped me bring a tighter focus to the message and were patient supporters while I recovered from open-heart surgery shortly after the project was initiated.

I must also recognize Mike Hagenhoff, Larry Porschen and the other leaders of the McBride Alumni Association who work hard to give forward to young men pursuing an education that embraces the teaching of Jesus Christ. These thousands of men have been my brothers for more than fifty years, and their friendship and brotherhood are gifts that will always be of great value to me.

My classmate and friend William (Bill) Genova holds a special place in my heart. He works diligently to keep us connected in prayer and service to one another. He is a man with a very generous heart.

There is not enough space to acknowledge all the people who have impacted my life these past seventy years, and their names, absent from these pages, remain imprinted on my heart. Their gifts of friendship, example and steadfastness have inspired me in periods of challenge. Three individuals are notable in standing with me during such times over the past 20 years: Dave Hefler, Fran Turbok and Carl Way. These individuals peered with me into the uncertainty of the 2001 dot com crash, the 2008-2009 financial crisis, and the Covid-19 challenge of 2020. Their support has been of immeasurable significance to me in those times.

I cannot underestimate the importance of family. My parents, grandparents, aunts, uncles, and cousins weaved the fabric of family into my being, and all contributed to my development. Special thanks to my grandmother, Josephine Pingsterhaus, who taught me that, "The key to a happy life is a generous heart." Also, I would be remiss if I did not mention my aunt, Maryann Haar, who embodied the principle of "family first." In times of challenge, she was always there supporting her sister, my mother. During challenging times, she always rose to the occasion. Finally, I thank my brother Mike for working hard to be a good man.

My children, Anne, Kate, Joe, and David, inspired me to discover my full potential. Providing them with the opportunity to grow and be productive contributors had me strive to consistently give them my very best effort.

My blessings were made complete by my wife, Jane. We are navigating the forty-fourth year of marriage, a journey that has led us into storms, navigating the rocks and shoals of life together. Her love, commitment and sacrifice have given me the strength to face adversity and the motivation to prevail. She taught me that loving someone requires that you put all your chips on the table and that our relationship is an all-in commitment in both times of challenge and success. She has helped me become a better man.

My life has been filled with individuals who strive to embrace the teachings of Jesus Christ. The message is simple: "Love one another;" and, "Do unto others as you would have them do unto you." My wish for you is to embrace His teachings and live a fuller life.

God Bless You!

ABOUT THE AUTHOR

Joseph Nettemeyer is a servant-leader, husband, father, accomplished businessman, and author of *Esto Vir: Be A Man*.

With over seventy years of life experience, Joe shares his stories of growing up in a family that didn't have much money but knew the importance of God and family.

With a no-excuse attitude coupled with loving grace, Joe shares the importance of trusting in God and taking responsibility of life, no matter what turn it may take. He has a passion for providing opportunities to young men and women to gain an education. He feels that with knowledge, anyone has an opportunity to succeed in life.

Joe and his wife have established schools for the ultra-poor in Bangladesh, sponsored scholarships to underprivileged children across the United States, and he has mentored hundreds of young men through the early years of their careers. For a "poor, south St. Louis boy just trying to make a living," his hard work, no-excuse attitude, and charitable works have impacted thousands of lives.

www.ingramcontent.com/pod-product-compliance
Lightning Source LLC
Chambersburg PA
CBHW072145090426
42739CB00013B/3287